POETRY CORNER

Cartoons by
NEIL BENNETT

Clare E. Hews illustrated by
MIKKI RAINE

Additional drawings
SCARFE, RUSHTON, NEWMAN

Published in Great Britain
by Private Eye Productions Ltd
6 Carlisle Street, London W1V 5RG
in association with Corgi Books
© 1992 Pressdram Ltd
ISBN 0 552 139971

Designed by Bridget Tisdall

Printed in Great Britain by
The Bath Press, Bath, Avon
Corgi Books are published by Transworld Publishers Ltd
61-63 Uxbridge Road, Ealing, London W5 5SA
in Australia by Transworld Publishers (Australia) Pty, Ltd
15-23 Helles Avenue, Moorebank, NSW 2170
and in New Zealand by Transworld Publishers (N.Z.) Ltd
Cnr Moselle and Waipareira Avenues, Henderson, Auckland

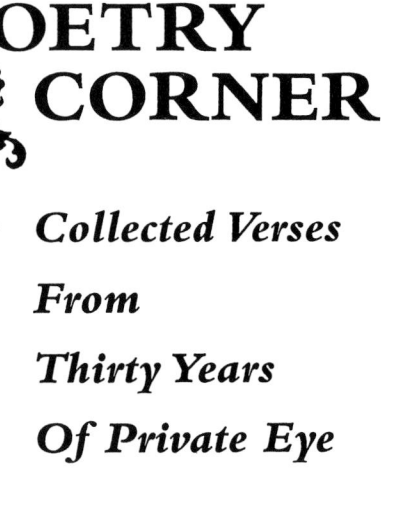

POETRY CORNER

Collected Verses
From
Thirty Years
Of Private Eye

PRIVATE EYE · CORGI

"It's desperate, sir – we're down to our last poet!"

ODE ON THE SOLEMN SEPARATION OF H.R.H. PRINCESS MARGARET & THE EARL OF SNOWDON, BY THE POET LAUREATE, SIR JOHN BETJEPERSON

Gosh, oh dear! What jolly bad luck!
Poor old Tony, and Margaret too.
Their nuptial bliss has come unstuck,
It seems the "arrangement" has fallen through.

I wonder what Brenda will have to say,
Back in the Palace over tea.
I expect there'll be all hell to pay,
I'm jolly glad it isn't me!

Poor little kiddies, off to Bedales —
Who's going to tell them, will it be Granny?
It might be their uncle, the Prince of Wales,
Or dear old Crawfie, the Royal Nanny!

On the 8.15 from Sidcup and Slough,
There's only one topic of conversation.
Who will they both get off with now?
At least, it makes a change from inflation!

Cheerio, old beans!

J.B.

Yes, It's House of Lords Rhyming Slang!

Apples and pears	**Kicked upstairs**
Rabid dog	**Quintin Hogg**
Face is red	**Lord Belstead**
Cledwyn-Hughes	**Booze**
Gentlemen's Relish	**Lord Mellish**
Lord Wilson of Rievaulx	**Give the heave-ho**
Lord Kagan	**Worse than Fagin**
Lord Home	**Darkened room**
Hear, hear	**Baroness Sear**
Lord Bonham-Carter	**Bit of a non-starter**
Long drone	**Baroness Blackstone**
Lord Mackay of Clashfern	**How much does he earn?**
Black Rod	**Silly old sod**

IN MEMORIAM

Sir Francis Chichester

So, old shipmate, you
Have finally set out again
Leaving a wife behind
Who you have so often left behind before.

Farewell then, old salt
Ancient mariner of a million voyages
Lone yachtsman we will
Remember your epic voyages

That helped to put Britain back on the
                                    map.
Oh lean bronzed man of the sea
With your spectacles and funny hat
You have sailed from our midst
But remain in our hearts
Oh wizened one.

Incidentally I see the job of Poet Laureate
Is still vacant. Far be it
From me to push myself forward
But such a post has always appealed
It can now be revealed.
(Just to show I can rhyme
As well as Sir J. Betjeman for example.)

Anyway, there it is. I'd be
Quite happy to do it
But there again, I won't mind if I don't.
I shall go on writing my poems
In either case.

By the way the address has
Changed of recent weeks.
I have left the Polytechnic
And may be contacted
c/o Mrs D. Norris Tiptree Woods
Herts.

E.J. Thribb (17)

Lines on the Engagement of David Frost & Diahann

Well done David and Diahann!
I hope that's the way you
Spell your name incidentally.
So you will be joined
Together in Holy Matrimony
At long last.

David Frost!
I used to think
You were terrific
On TW3 in the old days
I hope you won't mind
If I say that in more
Recent times Keith and I
(He's one of my mates) have gone
Off you and we think
Monty Python's much better.

Anyway no hard feelings I hope.
But you've got to speak
Your mind haven't you?
It's no use keeping these
Things bottled up.
After all you made your name
By being outspoken.

E.J. Thribb (17)

Clare E. Hew

William Burroughs
Has a face lined with furrows
Both his Jewish and Goy friends
Blame it on too many drugs and boy friends.

In Memoriam

Betty Grable

So. Farewell then
Betty, fabulous star
Of the fifties. Your
Legs were once
Insured for a
Million pounds
And you were the
Most popular
Pin Up of your
Day.

But beauty fades
Alas like the
Summer rose.

Personally I never
Saw your films.
But Keith's Mum
Who belongs to
An older generation
Saw every one.

E. JARVIS THRIBB (17)

An Ode On The Departure Of Sir Alec Douglas-Home

Penned in tearful farewell to a great statesman
by William McGonagall

'Twas in the year 1974
That Sir Alec Douglas-Home said he would stand no more
As Member of Parliament for Perthshire and Kinross
And to all of us it will be a great loss.

For Baillie, as the great laird is known,
To a ripe old age has nobly grown
And now before it is too late,
He is planning to devote himself to the affairs of his estate.

On the banks and braes of his native Tweed
His ghillies all wish him "God speed"
And many more things they'll stand there wishing
As they watch Sir Alec fishing.

As Lord Dunglass Sir Alec first came to fame
Working for Neville Chamberlain.
To Munich they flew in an aeroplane
And a few days later they flew back again.

It was not until 1955
That they discovered Sir Alec was still alive
And he became Secretary of State for Commonwealth Relations
In charge of the affairs of many diverse nations.

Being Foreign Secretary was Sir Alec's next job
Because Mr Macmillan was such a great snob.
He gave other jobs to many a lord
To represent him both at home and abroad.

Then Mr Macmillan fell ill, alas,
And to succeed him the Queen chose Baillie Vass.
Throughout the land the crowds cried "Amen"
To see a real gentleman at Number Ten.

But scarcely had he entered Downing Street
When he suffered his first major defeat
And lost the 1964 General Election
Because Harold Wilson was the country's first selection.

Shortly after that, in 1965,
Mr Heath became the leading Conservative,
And everyone thought Sir Alec's day was done
And that he would retire – his estates to run.

It was not to be, for in Mr Heath's first administration,
Sir Alec returned, to help rule the nation,
For now the people had come to see
What a wise and respected elder statesman was he.

But now at the ripe old age of 71
He has rightly decided his day is done
And so he retires to his ancestral house
To spend his time killing yon bonny grouse.

God rest you Baillie, now at last,
Your long and honourable career is past.
We'll confess we never quite understood how you got to the top
For it has to be said that in everything you did you were a terrible flop.

W. McGonagall

Lines written on the occasion of the return to his native land of Mr W. H. Auden

Welcome back, old bard,
With your craggy face, etched by
A million lines, and a cigarette
Between your lips. Dangling. So
You've come home again, have you
To spend
The twilight of your days
In a little cottage in Oxford.
(You were lucky to find a little place
                                    like that
Incidentally
With property prices rocketing up as
                                    they are
Due to the M4 and other factors.)

How we all remember that day in 1939
When you sailed away to America
(Or rather some of us don't because we
Were too young. I myself wasn't born
Till 1947, but that's
Beside the point).

Anyway, great to see you back
And I'm sure we all wish you a happy
Retirement, among the dreaming spires
And that.
What a pity by the way you didn't
Make it back sooner.
Then you might have been Poet Laureate
Instead of that bloke they've got at the
                        moment, what's his name?
You know the one.
I've never been one for names.

E.J. Thribb (16)

Yes, It's Church of England Rhyming Slang!

C of E	**Cup of tea**
Canterbury	**Glass of sherry**
Robert Runcie	**Duncie**
General Synod	**Don't believe in God**
Morning Prayer	**No one there**
Archbishop of York	**Nothing but talk**
Bishop of London	**Flies are undone**
Westminster Abbey	**Shabby**
Evensong	**Far too long**
1662	**Empty pew**
Selwyn Gummer	**Bummer**
Vicar of Bray	**Non-practising gay**
Women priests	**Dirty beasts**

LINES ON THE DEATH OF BILL HALEY

So. Farewell
Then Bill
Haley.

Founder of
Rock and
Roll.

One two three
O'clock four
O'clock Rock
Five six seven
            o'clock
Eight o'clock
Rock.

There is
    unfortunately
Not the space

Available to
Do full justice
to
Your Hit

Of many
Years ago.

E.J. Thribb (17)

In Memoriam

HENRY HALL
Bandleader

So. Farewell
Then
Henry Hall

Famous danceband
Leader of the
20s.

And star of
Radio.

"This *is*
Henry Hall
Speaking."

That was your
Catchphrase.

As catchphrases
Go,
It leaves
A lot

To be
Desired.

Still, Keith's Mum
Loves your
Hit record

Teddy Bears'
Picnic.

This *is*
E.J. Thribb
Writing.

Here's to
The next
Time.

E.J. Thribb (17½)

Yes, It's Garrick Club Rhyming Slang!

Game pie	**Club tie**
Large sherry	**Perry**
Change at Swindon	**Donald Sinden**
William Rees-Mogg	**Where's the bog?**
Brown Windsor Soup	**Worsthorne's got a scoop**
Extra strong mint	**Dirty Don's bint**
Oscar Beusalink	**Have another drink**
Trelford on Snooker	**Hooker**
Insulated loft	**Geoffrey Wheatcroft**
Sir Robin Day	**Gay**
Choice of gravies	**Justice Michael Davies**

ALBATROSS
à L'ORANGE
with
SLIMY
THINGS

LINES WRITTEN ON THE PASSING OF LORD HOLFORD

by SIR JOHN BETJEPERSON

Poor old Lord Holford! Gone at last to meet his Maker.
Ring out the bells from Paul's proud steeple
No more the matchbox blocks on every acre
Rising to dwarf us poor old ordinary people!

Father of Town and Country Planning legislation,
(According to *cp*, your buildings weren't so hot)
In country and town, it's time for celebration
You've placed upon the landscape your last blot!

(Not very good, is it? But I've got to go off to Cornwall now. Cheerio! J.B.)

In Memoriam
**Sir Alec Issigonis,
Auto Engineer**

So. Farewell
Then
Sir Alec
Issigonis.

Inventor of
The Mini.

"Mounting the engine
Transversely across
The Frame,

"And driving
The front wheels
Through an integral
Transmission."

Yes, that was
Your catchphrase.

Sir Eric J. Thribb (17½)

Clare E. Hew

His father's name is
A help to Martin Amis
And even more
To Auberon Waugh.

In Memoriam

Xavier Cugat
Bandleader

So. Farewell
Then

Xavier Cugat

King of Latin
American dance
Music.

Aye aye aye
Aye.

Cha cha
Cha.

Arrrrrimba.

Yes, those were
Your catchphrases.

Somehow, on the
Page they
Do not capture

The magic
Of the
Rumba.

E.J. Thribb (17½)

Yes, It's Sandie Shaw Rhyming Slang!

Sandie Shaw	**Sixties bore**
No shoes	**Old news**
Bare feet	**Repeat**
Same again	**Buddhist, Zen**
Aged 44	**Another encore**
Dated look	**Written a book**
"World at my feet"	**Rubbish (complete)**
Exclusive interviews	**Snooze**
Dagenham-born	**Yawn**
Jeff Banks	**No thanks**
Puppet On A String	**Couldn't sing**

In Memoriam
Lines on the Death of
A.J.P. Taylor, Historian
and Television
Personality

So. Farewell
Then
A.J.P. Taylor

Historian and
Television Personality.

Keith's mum
Remembers you
On the Telly

In your
Bowtie,
Making it up
As you
Went along.

Now, you
Are history
As well.

E.J.P. Thribb (17½)

In Memoriam
Charles Atlas

Farewell mighty muscle man!
You of the bulging biceps
And titanic torso.
It doesn't matter how strong
You are. You have to die
In the end.

Actually I sent off
For one of your dynamic
Tension kits once when I was at
School. But it had
No effect
That I could detect.

I remained, in your
Language, a seven
Stone weakling.

But speaking as a poet
What use are rippling muscles
And tip-top physique?
Bodily strength is not necessary
In the writing of poetry
Witness all the great poets
From Homer to the present day.
Many of them were puny specimens
Looked at from a purely physical
Point of view.

My mate Keith points out
That many of my poems
Of late have concerned
The passing on of Great Men
And it is time for a change.
Alas! Poetic inspiration
Is not something you can control
Like prices and incomes.

But Keith does not see
This.

Eric Jarvis Thribb (17)

Clare E. Hew

Syvia Plath
Belonged in the W.R.A.F.
Air Vice-Marshal Audrey Twining
Would have put a stop to her whining.

Charles Atlas

Lines Written on the Nuptials of H.R.H. the Prince of Wales & Lady Lavinia Tharg

(Please check, old bean, I may have got the name wrong. J.B.)

by Sir John Betjeperson

From Uxbridge and from Potters Bar
    From Morden and from Kew
See them come from near and far
    To get a royal view.

It might look better on the telly
    Sitting cosily at home
With Uncle Bert and Auntie Nellie
    And cousin Archie up from Frome.

But nothing beats the crowded pavement
    Here on leafy Ludgate Hill
Now we know what 'royal wave' meant —
    Golly, what a real thrill!

Look they're coming! Clip, clop, clap,
    Horses, coaches, soldiers gay.
Quick now, granny, take your snap,
    While we all shout 'Hip, hurray!'

Here comes Brenda, don't you love her?
    Looking radiant in her crown.
Here's our wonderful Queen Mother,
    Back from Bognor looking brown.

And isn't that the King of Tonga
　　With his laundry on his head?
But I can't stand here any longer
　　After my nineteen weeks in bed.

Come inside, where they're all waiting
　　For the coming of the bride.
Notice that old wrought-iron grating
　　Put up by Sir Makepeace Gryde.[1]

Ring out the bells in jubilation,
　　Now they're well and truly hitched.
Not since Brenda's coronation
　　Have we all been so bewitched.

Let the beacons blaze their message
　　From Uffington to Wenlock Edge,
From Shepton Mallet up to Cressage
　　(That's in Salop, I allege).

But as we all carouse and wassail
　　To celebrate this glorious day,
In tower block and ducal castle
　　Drinking half the night away

Spare a thought for one old lady,
　　Sitting all alone and glum;
Couldn't get a cheap away-day
　　So she said she couldn't come.

Barbara Cartland, don't you love her,
　　With her feather-boa'd hat.
Lady Dartmouth's dear old mother,
　　All of eighty — fancy that!

(It's not awfully good, is it? Put it in if you like — just off to Padstow. Cheerio! J.B.)

[1] No one remembers him now but in his day he was highly regarded as an ecclesiastical architect and he also built the National Westminster Bank in Castle Cary.

THE AMADEUS STRING QUARTET

1948-1973

So. You have been playing
Together for 25 years.
That's a terrifically
Long time when
You think how many other
Groups break up
After only a few months
Or even less.

Greetings, then, maestri,
(I hope that is correct)
You must feel
Quite chuffed having
Lasted so long.

Norbert Brainin and Siegmund
Nissel (violins): Peter Schidlof
(viola), Martin Lovett (cello)
How often have those
Names been heard by
Music lovers read out
On the radio.

Norbert. That has always
Struck me as a curious
Name.

My mate Keith
Does not seem to
Appreciate classical
Music. I've tried
To explain
Why people go to
Listen to it. But
He cannot understand.
Whenever I go round to
His place he has
Always got heavy rock
Like Crosby Stills & Nash
On the stereo.

Ah well. It takes all
Sorts I suppose.

E J THRIBB (17)

Clare E. Hew

FrancisBacon
Is not a Jamaican;
It's his only link
With Elizabeth Frink.

Lines on the Death of Dr Beeching

So. Farewell
Then Dr
Beeching.

Yes, you were
The man who
Axed the
Railways.

Now you too
Have been
Axed in
Your turn.

It happens
To us all.

E. J. Thribb (17)

LINES ON THE VISIT TO BRITAIN OF THE DALAI LAMA

Hello, Dalai!
(No disrespect
Intended.) You are
Here from the
Mysterious
Country on the
Roof of the World
About which so
Little is known
Even now.

You are a great
Spiritual leader
With your bald
Head and sari.
To hundreds of
People in your
Native Tibet
You are God
Incarnate.

Dalai Lama.
The name itself
Is strange.
Keith's mum however
Confused you with
The Abominable
      Snowman.

E.J. Thribb (17)

Yes, It's Law Courts Rhyming Slang!

Enormous fee	Top QC
Silence in court	Gone for a snort
Court of Appeal	Garrick Club meal
Bundle B	Time for a pee
Majesty of the Law	Knock off at four
Lord Lane	Wrong again
Vintage Port	Contempt of court
Carter Ruck	EXPLETIVE DELETED
Fudge	Judge
Justice Michael Davies	Rabies
M'Learned Friend	Money to spend
Smoked Salmon sandwiches	Aggravated damages
Writ	EXPLETIVE DELETED
Justice Popplewell	Extremely good man

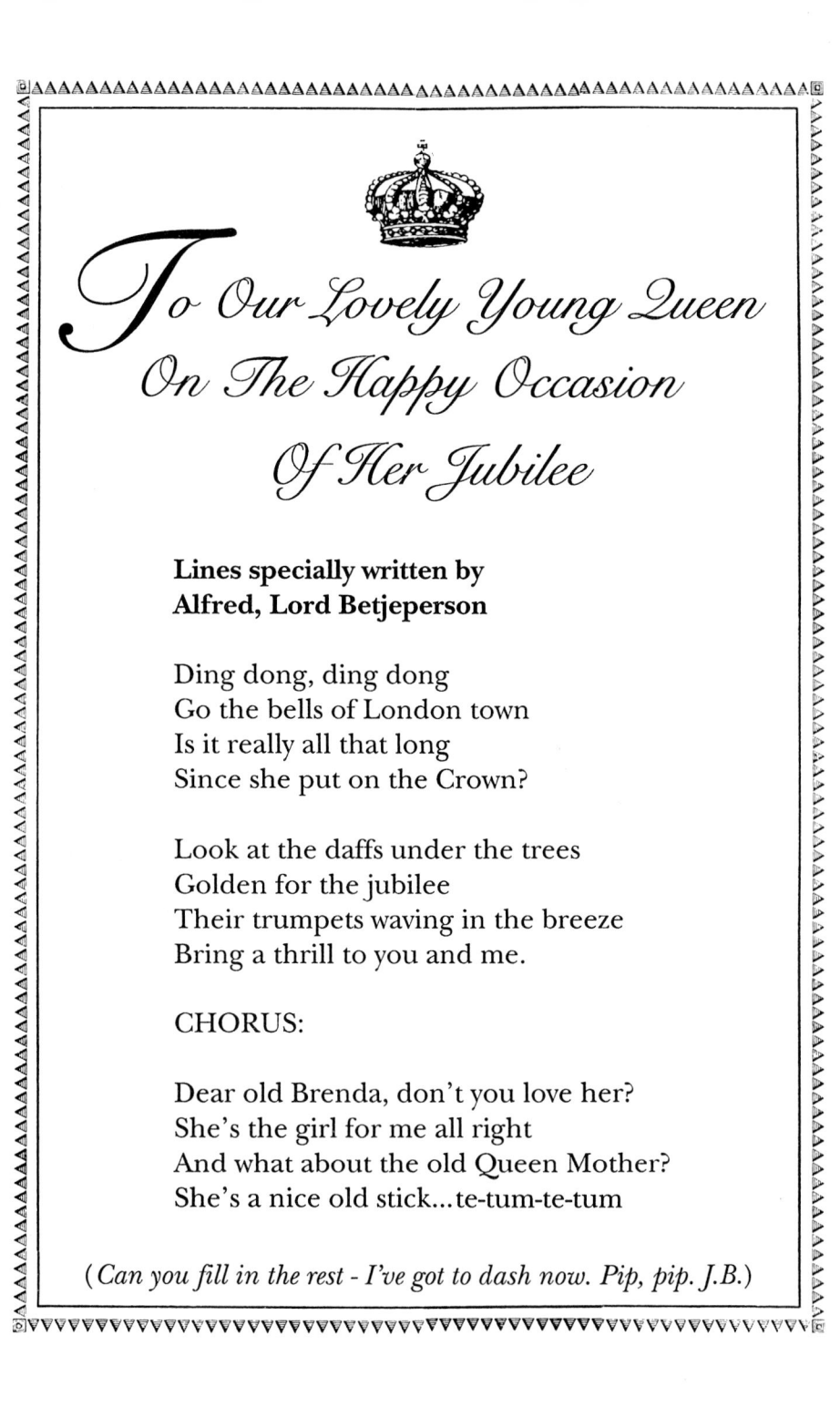

To Our Lovely Young Queen On The Happy Occasion Of Her Jubilee

Lines specially written by
Alfred, Lord Betjeperson

Ding dong, ding dong
Go the bells of London town
Is it really all that long
Since she put on the Crown?

Look at the daffs under the trees
Golden for the jubilee
Their trumpets waving in the breeze
Bring a thrill to you and me.

CHORUS:

Dear old Brenda, don't you love her?
She's the girl for me all right
And what about the old Queen Mother?
She's a nice old stick...te-tum-te-tum

(Can you fill in the rest - I've got to dash now. Pip, pip. J.B.)

Franco
1892–1972

Olé! Il Generale!
So, you are eighty today
And working at your desk
As usual.

You are the last of the
Great ones. Churchill
De Gaulle and Stalin.
It seems extraordinary
Really that you still
Hold office.

Spain.
Land of señoritas and castanets
Blood-red Chianti
And the age-old ritual of
The Bull-fight.
Yes! What a fantastic place!
Bravo, Amigo!
Multi salutos (I hope that's right)

Apparently, according to my mate
                                    Keith
You are a dictator
Employing brutal police who walk
About telling holiday-makers
Not to wear bikinis.

That may be so
But it is not for me
To go into that kind of question
In a poem.

E.J. Thribb (17)

In Memoriam
Anton Karas

So. Farewell then
Anton Karas.
Yes, we remember you.
You composed the
Third Man Theme
And played it on your
Zither.

Dum-de-dum-de-dum
De-dum.
Dum-de-dum-de-dum
De-dum.
Dum-ti-tee-ti-tee-ti-tee
De-dum.

And so on.

E.J. Thribb (17)

Clare E. Hew

If you haven't read Gissing
You don't know what you're missing:
Endless novels
About whores in hovels.

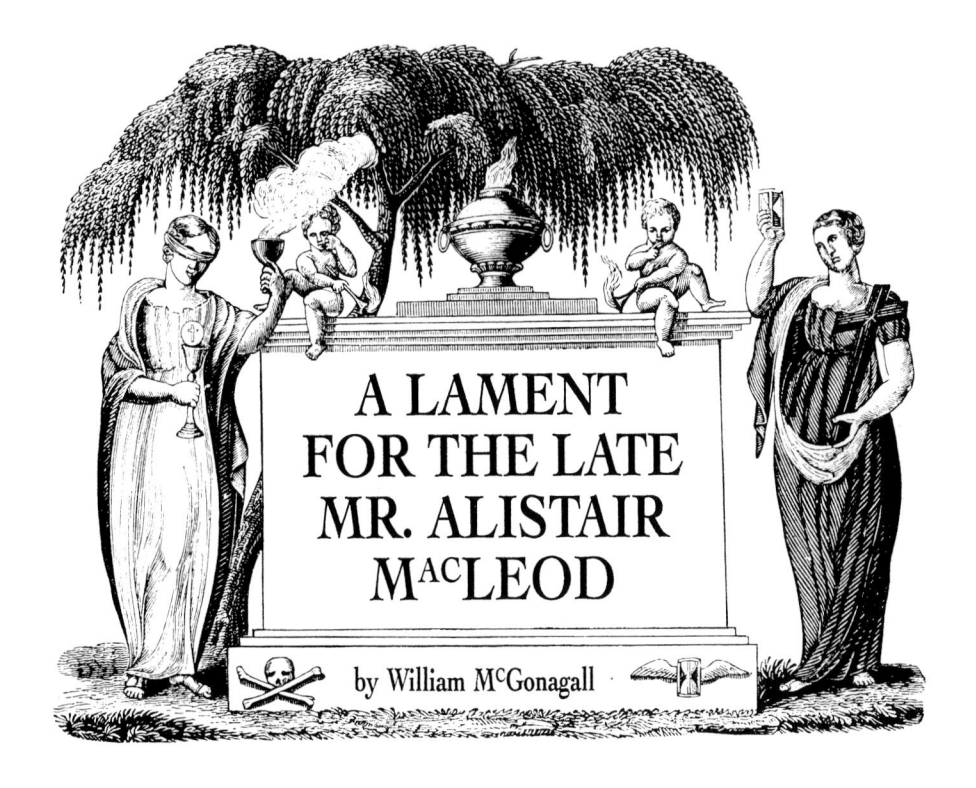

A LAMENT FOR THE LATE MR. ALISTAIR M^{AC}LEOD

by William McGonagall

It was in the year nineteen hundred and seventy-eight
That by the banks of the famous River Plate
Eleven braw laddies frae bonnie Scotland
Arrived in Argentina, that far-off hot land.
By land and by sea came hundreds of fans
Representing all the different clans —
Campbells, Macdonalds, Douglas-Homes,
All giving off a variety of appalling fumes.
With raucous voices they sang aloud
The praises of their great leader, MR ALLY MacLEOD.
"We are Ally's Army," they all sang with one accord,
"And when Ally wins, they will make him a Lord."
Meanwhile Mr MacLeod told the press what he would do,

"We'll gang out there on Saturday and walk all o'er Peru."
For this was the side they had to face
In the first stage of their long and arduous race.
And so the great day came to pass
When Ally's men ran out on that newly-mown grass
To face the team from the land of Inca
And, alas to relate, they pulled a stinker.
To behold the score, three goals to one,
For the Scottish fans was not much fun.
But the brave MacLeod was in no way dismayed,
Saying, "There are still two more games to be played."
The next game was against Iran
(Or Persia, as it would be known to an older man).
Scoffed Ally, "These boogers will not even score,"
But to everyone's surprise Scotland were held to a one-all draw
(And even the goal that the Scots lads made
Was of the type that Pevsner would have played).
Never had there been such a day of disgrace
In the whole history of the proud Scottish race.
And to add to all the rest of their shame
Came the news that Willie Johnston would be sent hame
(For in order to increase his natural zest
He had taken a pill and failed his test).
Then no one had any longer a good word for Ally
But of every journalist he became the Aunt Sally.
And as for the fans who had travelled to the Argentine,
They turned on their hero and gave him the V-sign.
And so were dashed the hopes of Ally MacLeod,
A man now crushed who was once so proud.
His total humiliation from Scotland's day of shame was such
That it did not even matter when they beat the Dutch.

In memoriam Palden Thondup Namgyal formerly King of Sikkim

So. Farewell
Then Palden
Thondup
Namgyal
Formerly
King of
Sikkim.

I have
Copied your
Name from
The *Guardian*.

Keith says
This is no
Guarantee of
Accuracy.

But even so
It is a
Strange name

Whichever
Way it is
Spelled.

E. Thondup Thribbyal (17)

Yes, It's Francis Bacon Rhyming Slang!

Greatest painter since Turner	Nice little earner
Screaming Pope	Money for old rope
Triptych	Makes you sick
Anal fixation	Bought for the nation
Self-hate	In the Tate
Seedy Soho life	Never had a wife
Dinner at the Ritz	Not keen on tits
Images of violent sex	Enormous cheques
Writhing torso	The same, only more so
Francis Bacon	Godforsaken

Clare E. Hew

Carl Gustav Jung
Was very well hung.
A fact which annoyed
Sigmund Freud.

IN MEMORIAM VLADIMIR NABOKOV

So. Farewell
Then Vladimir
Nabokov.

Author of *Lolita*
A name that
Has passed into
The language.

You read in
The paper of
"Lolita girl
in Love Drama"
For example.

Yet how
Many people
I wonder
Have read
The original book?

I have not
For one.

It is not the
Type of book
That interests me

Particularly.

  E Jarvis-Thribb (17)

"I shot this morning's minion, Mr 'opkins"

Lines on the award "Pipe Man of the Year" to Magnus Magnusson

So. Magnus
Magnusson.

You are the
"Pipeman of
The Year".

Pipeman.
A curious title.

How do you
Win?

Surely not
Just by
Smoking a
Pipe?

There would
Have to be more
To it than that.

Or would there?

  E. Jarvis Thribb (17)

Lines on the Deaths of John Wayne and Norman Hartnell

So farewell then
John Wayne and
Norman Hartnell.

Cowboy and
Royal couturier.

You could not
be more
different.

You John Wayne
With your six guns
And big hat

You Norman Hartnell
Designing dresses
For Royal occasions

No. I can
Think of
Nothing whatsoever

That you
Could be said
To have in
Common

E. Jarvis Thribb (17)

Clare E. Hew

Mr David Irving
Is utterly unswerving
In his dedication
To the Aryan nation.

In Memoriam

The Master
(1900-1973)

So. The curtain has come
Down at last on
Your highly successful
Career as playwright,
Song-writer, performer,
What you will.

To my mind you
Epitomised the highly
Sophisticated night
Life of Theatre World.

Farewell then
Sir Noel!
With your long cigarette
                    holder and
Silk Dressing Gown
You had style —
That indefinable something
Which has gone forever
Out of our life.

Keith's mum apparently
Can remember seeing
You in the Vortex.
But I believe
They've pulled
That pub down now.

ERIC JARVIS THRIBB (17)

Lines on the Unmasking of the Surveyor of the Queen's Pictures

by The Poet Laureate
Sir Jawn Bargeperson

Poor old Bluntie! So they got him,
"Mole Revealed" they say "at last".
On a bleak November morning,
What an echo from the past!

Old Marlburian, I recall him,
In his flannel bags and hat
Wandering by the River Talbot,
Sometimes straining at a gnat.

Who'd have guessed it — "Blunt a traitor"
And an homosexualist?
Carrying on with Tar and waiter —
There's a sight I'm glad I missed.

Now the nine day wonder's over
Back he goes to Maida Vale,
In his comfy little Rover —
Home to gin and ginger ale.

Was it worth it? Does it matter?
In the end we do not know.
Now I'm madder than a hatter,
Goodness me! It's time to go.

(Put it in if you like it. It is not very good, is it? J.B.)

They say that the Runcies
Are absolute dunces
But that's all right
Not many clergymen or their wives
    are particularly bright.

Lines on the death of John Bodkin Adams

So. Farewell
Then John
Bodkin Adams,

Yes,
You bumped off
A lot of rich
Old ladies

On the South Coast
And got away with it.

I can say
That now

Because you are
Dead and so
Unable to sue.

E. Jarvis Thribb (17)

In Memoriam Larry Parnes
("Mr Parnes Shillings and Pence")

So. Farewell
Then
Larry Parnes

Pop impresario.

Yes, you
Discovered Dicky Pride,
Johnny Gentle, Vince
Eager, Marty Wilde
And Tommy Steele.

"I'll make you
A star."

That was
Your catchphrase.

"Where's my
Money?"

That was
Theirs.

E. J. Thribb (17)

Lines on the raising of the
MARY ROSE

by William McGonagall

'Twas in the year nineteen hundred and eighty-two,
When *Mary Rose* was brought up from the ocean for all to view.
For four hundred years she had lain at the bottom of the Solent.
For Alexander McKee it was certainly a great moment.

Since nineteen sixty-two Mr McKee made it his utmost endeavour
Diving to the deep in all kinds of weather
To raise Henry VIII's flagship the *Mary Rose*,
Giving up well-earned hours of sweet repose

His Royal Highness the Prince of Wales also took a great interest,
Personally diving down to inspect the wreck in his black rubber vest.
The bonny Prince lent his name to the Charitable Trust,
Which eventually raised £4 million so Mr McKee wouldn't go bust.

Intense was the excitement when the great day dawned.
But soon it fell out that the TV viewers yawned
As the great operation had to be delayed
Due to technical difficulties, so it was said.

But at last on October 11 at the stroke of nine
The giant lifting crane Tog Moor began to pull on her line
And slowly the great flagship appeared,
Then everyone on the quayside clapped and cheered.

Church bells rang out from far and near
And the guns saluted their ancient peer.
Archaeologist Margaret Rule could not
                          contain her joy,
And Prince Charles smiled like a wee
                          bairn with a new toy.

But to everyone else it was a sorry sight:
A lot of old planks of wood that could
                          not be set alight.
So they towed to Portsmouth this old
                          wreck so rotten
And by the end of the day the *Mary Rose*
                          had been quite forgotten.

©1982 W. McGonagall

Lines on the Return to the BBC of David Coleman

So. David Coleman
You are coming
Back.

Many people
Think of you
As the Number
One Sports
Commentator.

Where have you
Been these last
Months?

What does a
Commentator do
When he is
Not commentating?

You
Sit at home
Perhaps. Watching
TV.

Thinking of the
Things you
Might say

If you were
There.

To remain silent
When it's a goal
Must be difficult.

You must want
To shout something.

"It's a goal!"
Perhaps.

E.J. Thribb (17)

Clare E. Hew

Mr Norman Tebbit
Has one thing to his debit
Even though he's a Government Minister
He can't help looking dreadfully
unattractive and sinister.

Yes, It's Ken Russell Rhyming Slang!

Whore	**Terrific bore**
Women In Love	**See above**
Russell, Ken	**Same again**
Bartok	**Load of cock**
Bio pics	**Naked pricks**
Inspired cutting	**Lots of rutting**
Gothic	**Even more dick**
Liszt	**One to be missed**
Elgar	**Worst by far**
Compared to Orson Welles	**Pull the other one, it's got bells**

Lines on the Wimbledon Victory in the Women's Singles of Virginia Wade

Quiet please!

So. Congratulations
Then Virginia
Wade

Or Ginny as
You are better
Known in
The popular
Press.

For years you
Have struggled
To achieve
This goal.

Now in Jubilee
Year in the
Presence of Her
Majesty the
Queen you
Have at last
Succeeded.

4 – 6
6 – 3
6 – 1

These simple
Figures do not
Tell the whole
Story

But there is
Not enough room
In a poem for
Anything more
Specific.

E. Jervase Thribb (17)

"I suppose you're the last of the big Spenders"

In Memoriam
Donald Peers

So, popular singer,
The music has
Faded on the air
Leaving behind
An eerie silence.

Personally I am too
Young to remember
The tunes that
Endeared you to
The hearts of
Millions.

Normally I would
Ask Keith's mum
To give me the
Relevant information

But
She is away
With her sister
In Frinton
And will not
Be back
For two weeks.

ERIC JARVIS-THRIBB (17)

Clare E. Hew

PhilipLarkin
Willneverhavetroubleparkin'.
Heisthegreatestpoetalive
Whocannotdrive.

In Memoriam
Salvador Dali
Master of Surrealism

So.
Hello then
Dali.

You are
A
Fish.

Keith's Mum
Is
Melting.

E.J. Watch (17)

IN MEMORIAM

Krishna Menon

So Farewell Krishna
Menon.

Krishna. That
Is familiar on
Account of the members of the
Exotic Religions sect with

Shaven heads and
Clashing Cymbals

Who can be seen
Dancing through the
Streets. A strange
Spectacle.

Whence do they come?
Whither do they go?

(Personally I would not
Like to have my
Head shaven when
The weather's like this.)

E.J. Thribb (17)

Yes, It's TUC Rhyming Slang!

Carthorse	**Spent Force**
TUC	**Not for me**
Ron Todd	**Thinks he's God**
NUM	**No support for them**
Norman Willis	**That's what a pill is**
Bit of a laugh	**Rodney Bickerstaffe**
Political levy	**Who's for a bevvy?**
Pint of stout	**All out**
Sam McLuskey	**Treble whuskey**
New Agenda	**Go on a bender**
Union subs	**Blackpool clubs**
Len Murray	**Late night curry**
Onion bhaji	**Arthur Scargy**
TGWU	**Vindaloo**
Brothers and sisters	**Newts, as pissed as**

IN MEMORIAM
Chairman Mao

So.
Farewell then
Chairman Mao.

You are the
Last of the
Great revolutionary

Figures. You
And I
Had little in
Common

Except that
Like me
You were a poet.

Though how you
Found time
To write poems

In addition to
Running a
Country of
800 million people

Is baffling
Frankly.

E.J. Thribb (17)

In Memoriam
**Geoff Love,
Bandleader**

So. Farewell
Then, Geoff
Love.

Better known
As Manuel
And The Music
Of The
Mountains.

Geoff and
The Music
Of The Mountains.

No.
This would
Not have appealed
To Keith's
Mum.

E.J. Thribb (17½)

Clare E. Hew

Svetlana Stalin
Was Daddy's little darlin'.
She never went in for mass slaughter
But is otherwise truly his daughter.

Yes, It's Wimbledon Rhyming Slang!

Duchess of Kent	Corporate Tent
Serve and Volley	Drinks Trolley
Glass of Sherry	Des and Gerry
Sabatini	Dry Martini
Sue Mott	Not Very Hot
Dan Maskill	Worse than Ian McCaskill
Quiet Please	Huge Fees
Large Czech	Large Cheque
McEnroe	Time To Go
Navratilova	Lesbian Legover
Steffi Graf	Not Much of a Laugh
Strawberries and Cream	Price is Obscene
Boris Becker	Pain in the Necker
Stupid Grunt	Line-Judge

Lines on the Death of Maria von Trapp

So. Farewell
Then Maria
Von Trapp

Famous *Sound
Of Music* Lady.

Keith's Mum
Has seen
*The Sound of
Music* seventeen
Times.

"Climb Every
Mountain".
Yes,
That was
Your catchphrase.

*E.J. Thribb (sixteen
going on seventeen)*

Lines on the Retirement of the Speaking-Clock Lady from the GPO

• • • • • • • • • • • •

So. Farewell then
Miss Pat Simmons.

Although your name
Is perhaps not
Widely known

Your voice
Is familiar
To Millions

"At the third
Stroke it will
Be 10.43 –
Precisely."

Pip!
Pip!
Pip!

At the third
Stroke it will
Be 10.43
And ten seconds

And so on.

E. Jervase Thribb (17)

Lines on the Death of Lord Clark, Ex-King Idris of Libya and Sidney Box
(who he? Ed.)

So Farewell
Then. Lord Clark

You were best
Known for your
Programme on
Civilisation

"What could
Be more
Agreeable?"
That was your
Catchphrase

Idris. A
Strange name.

Keith's Mum
Recalls that
It was once

The name of
A Lemon Squash

I drinks
Idris

When I's
Dri

Was the
Slogan.

E. Dris Thribb (17)

Sir Jonah Betjeperson

Lines on the 80th Birthday of the Queen Mother

Everybody's favourite Granny
    It's your Birthday — Oh Hurray!
Here comes Charles and little Annie
    With their presents for today.

Here is Brenda with her parcel —
    What's inside? A nice new hat
All the way from Boutique Marcel;
    Philip's brought a "Welcome" mat.

Margaret's brought a crate of whisky
    'Cos she knows you like a drop,
Soon you'll both be feeling frisky,
    Once you start it's hard to stop.

On the pavement in St James's
    Crowds are waiting with their flags.
Couldn't tell you what their names is —
    "Here she comes! Put out your fags!"

"Look! She's waving from the window —
    Where's your Instamatic, Sid?"
I don't think I can write any more now
    Sorry about that — Cheerio, old bean!

Pip-Pip. J.B.

LINES WRITTEN BY THE POET LAUREATE ON LEARNING OF THE NEWS (SEVERAL WEEKS LATE) OF THE DEATH OF EARL MOUNTBATTEN OF BURMA

In the bright September sunshine,
See the sailors marching by.
Here they come from Deal and Reading,
Now the mighty crowd is heading
Down the Mall towards the Abbey,
Some are smart and some are shabby,
Some are thin and some are flabby.

Not much good, is it? But I only got back from Cornwall on Tuesday, and we haven't seen the *Telegraph* for weeks.
    Is it still coming out?
    Put it in if you like. I won't mind if you don't. Cheerio, old bean. Love to the missus. J.B.

Lines on the Overthrow of the Cambodian leader Pol Pot

So. Pol
Pot. You
Have been
Overthrown.

Pol Pot.
A strange
Name.

One of the
Strangest I
Have come
Across.

Join it
Together.

Polpot.

It is the
Kind of
Word they
Have on
*Call My
Bluff.*

E.J. Thribb (17)

In Memoriam

Roy Orbison

So.
Farewell then
Roy Orbison.

Or "Big
O" as you
Were known.

Sixties hit-maker,
We remember
You.

With your
Dark glasses
And three-octave
Range.

"Only The Lonely".
Yes. That was
A hit.

"Pretty Woman". That
Was another.

So was
"It's Over".

Which sadly is
The case.

E.J. Thribb (17½)

Clare E. Hew

They say Mrs Gandhi
Is terribly randy
But she doesn't talk much about it
And personally I doubt it.

Lines On The Opening Of The New Thames River Barrage

by Mr William McGonagall

'Twas in the year 1984, on the 8th May
That there dawned at last the glorious day
When the great Thames Barrier was complete —
A most remarkable engineering feat.

For hundreds of years Londoners had dwelled in dread
Scarcely able to sleep soundly in their bed
Lest at any moment the river should o'erflow
Leaving them all with nowhere to go.

So to avert this appalling disaster
Sir Desmond Plummer vowed that of the Thames he would
                                    become master.
(Sir Desmond was the Leader of the GLC,
Way back in nineteen seventy-three.)

For many a year the workmen toiled,
With honest labour their limbs were soiled.
Every day they laboured, whether rainy or sunny
Spending an enormous pile of the taxpayers' money

'Til finally, at a cost of 1000 million pound,
A mighty contraption rose from out of the ground —
Or perhaps closer to the truth it would be
To say that it rose from out of the sea.

And so down the Thames came a great armada:
The crowd of onlookers could not have cheered harder
As forth from the shadow of famous Big Ben
Came the Queen and the mother of little Red Ken.

The barge they sat in was of burnished gold
(A line that has already been written, so I am told).
They sailed past the City, Rotherhithe and Wapping —
The view they got of the tower blocks was simply topping.

To Greenwich they came, both the Queen and Ma Ken
Past the hospital built by Sir Christopher Wren
(Also to be seen there is the Cutty Sark
Adjacent to a very nice municipal park).

So at last they arrived at the magnificent barrier
Each section as big as an aircraft carrier
And there to greet them were many important men
But most famous of all was the great Red Ken.

Newt-lover and Monarch, at last face to face
The two greatest members of the British race.
Such a sight no one had been able to behold
Since Henry VIII met the King of France on the Field of the
Cloth of Gold.

Lines on the 80th Birthday of Alfred Hitchcock

So. Alfred
Hitchcock. You
Are 80.

Master of
Suspense as you
Have been called.

Keith says you are
Best known for
The fact

E.J. Thribb

That you always
Make a brief
Appearance in

Your own films.

I would like
To do the
Same in my
Poems.

But it looks
A bit odd
I think.

E.J. Thribb (17)

Yes, It's Royal Institute of British Architects Rhyming Slang!

Hi Tech	Enormous Cheque
Planning Consent	Money well spent
Peter Palumbo	Bit of a dumbo
Paternoster	Norman Foster
Sucks up to Hacks	Hutchinson, Max
Exciting Low Rise	Silly Bow Ties
Denis Lasdun	Look what he *has* done
Richard Rodgers	Bodgers
Service Ducts	Building sucks
James Stirling	Preferred Albert Speer's plan for Berlin
Glass of sherry	Quinlan Terry
Georgian pastiche	Nouveau Riche
Gavin Stamp	In the other camp

Lines on the Death of Pope John Paul I

So. Farewell then
Pope John Paul I
After only thirty-
Four days.

John Paul.
A name chosen
From

Your predecessors.

Keith suggests that
The next Pope
Should be
Called

John Paul George
And Ringo.

But I consider
That remark
Is in poor taste

Under the
        circumstances.

E.J. Thribb (17½)

Clare E. Hew

Cardinal O'Fiaich
(Who he?
Can't you do someone else instead?
Ed.)

Lines on the departure of John Nott MP

So Farewell
Then John
Nott Minister
of Defence

You are
Resigning
From Parliament

Nott the Minister
of Defence

Keith said
It sounded

Like a
Joke

By Rowan
Atkinson

E.J. Thribb (17)

Yes, It's Rudolf Nureyev Rhyming Slang!

Sugar Plum	Kicked colleague up bum
Ballet tights	Gets in fights
Death In Venice	Man's a menace
Giselle	To work with, hell
Slow on his feet	Nutcracker Suite
Dying Swan	Carried on too long
En l'air	Losing hair
Tub of lard	Scheherazade
Legs ache	Swan Lake
Pas de deux	Bit vieux
Romeo	Time to go
Kirov	Get him off
Don Quixote	Mr Kick-Bot (*You've had that, Ed.*)

Lines on the Retirement of Sir Robin Day from *Question Time*

So. Farewell
Then
Sir Robin
Day.

"Yes. The gentleman
In the red.
Yes, you
Sir. No,
Not you in
The glasses,
You, next
To the
Woman in blue."

That was
Your catchphrase.

E.J. Thribb (17½)

Clare E. Hew

Sir Basil Spence
Showed a great deal of sense
When he bought a house in Norfolk
As far away as he could get from the buildings
he designed for the rest of us poor folk.

**In Memoriam
Arnold Ridley**

So farewell
Then Arnold
Ridley

Of *Dad's Army*
Fame.

You were the
Old One

Who always
Wanted to go
To the toilet.

E.J. Thribb (17)

Lines on the 8oth Birthday of Fred Astaire

So. Fred
Astaire. You
Are eighty.

Congratulations
Great dancer.

Tap tap tap
Tappity
Tap te tap
Te tap tap.

It is difficult
To convey
In a poem

The peculiar
Magic of your

Immortal feet.

In your top
Hat and tails

You look
The epitome of
Elegance.

And yet
Remarkably
You chose
The name Fred

Rather than
Frederick.

Frederick Astaire.
I think personally
It sounds better.
(But it would be
Too late to change
It now.)

E. Jarvis Thribb (17)

Lines on the Christening of Prince Harry and the failure of HRH Princess Anne to attend the ceremony

by the new Poet Laureate
TED WHOHES

Under Balbooley crag
In an eddy of whirlpools
Flows

The Crow.
Black clouds crack
With thunder as
Old milk bottles
Bob, fizz, thunder
Under
The Crow

Scargill Moor
Mist-draped
Sheep wet, old trousers
Left to rot
And the Kerridge
Rising from beneath
Dark dungeons
Filled with white bones
Of dead
Crows
Surges down the side
Of Morecambe Fell
Dripping blood
From the shaggy pores
Of the dead sheep
Eddies gurgling over
Jags of polished bones

Detergent bottles
Twisting and writhing past
Rusty bedspreads
Strewn like giant
Crows

On old half-covered
Mouldy turnips
The stench of dying
Bleeding laughing
(*shome mishtake?*)
Rabbits hit the
Nostril like shrapnel
The stomach churns
Like the waters of
Gowrie Bilgarth
In the rainy season
When the dead fish
Drift half silver
Half green like
Crows
Down down down
Towards the Sunlit
Pool beneath Scar Mooly
Where the green slime
Coagulates in a film
Of brackish brown garbage
Will this do?

Ted W.

**Lines on the departure
of Mr Barry Took,
presenter of the BBC's**
Points of View

So. Farewell
Then
Barry Took.

You have
Been fired.

Keith's mum
Is most upset.

She once
Had a letter on

Saying how
Good the
BBC was.

E.J. Thribb (17)

Clare E. Hew

Pope John Paul the Second
Is generally reckoned
The kind of chap you want if
You're looking for a Pontiff.

In Memoriam
Greta Garbo, Goddess of the Silver Screen and Hollywood Enigma

So. Farewell
Then,
Greta Garbo.

Goddess of the
Silver screen

And Hollywood
Enigma.

I vant to
Be alone.

That was
Your catchphrase.

Perhaps it would
Have been better
To begin:
So. Farevell
Then.

Yes. I
Think it
Vorks.

E.J. Thribb (17½)

Yes, It's Royal Academy of Arts Summer Exhibition Rhyming Slang!

R.A.	More to pay
Anthony Green	Mildly obscene
Animal print	Makes a mint
Boardroom portrait	Fourth-rate
One to be missed	Abstract Expressionist
Catalogue	Bog
Reclining nude	Not much good
Little red sticker	Bought by a vicar
Casson, Sir Hugh	Not much of a queue
Peter Blake	Could be a fake
Not that great	Carel Weight
Couldn't be duller	Greek watercolour
Elizabeth Frink	Could do with a drink
Patricia O'Brien	You're right, I'm dying

LINES ON THE RETIREMENT OF MR RONALD BARKER

So.
Farewell then
Ronnie Barker

Of Two
Ronnies fame.

It Is Goodnight
From You,
But not Goodnight
From Him.

Keith's Mum
Says
The One Ronnie
Will not
Sound the same.

E.J. Thribb (17½)

Clare E. Hew

Elias Canetti
Has a passion for spaghetti.
When writing Auto da Fé
He ate it three times a day.

Lines on the Love-Affair between HRH Princess Michael of Kent and Texan millionaire J.R. Ewing

by Sir Tedwyn Whohes, Poet Laureate

Granite eyes flecked with
Steel the Owl sits.
Old Owly
Dark sentinel in the
Gruesome night

Old Owly waits

Then plunges down
Down down
(That's enough downs. Ed.)
Bone crushing claws
Tearing blood screaming

Old Owly swoops

Sleek-coat mouse
Blood dappled guts
Spewing dead eyes
Staring
Dead. Dead. Dead.
(That's enough deads. Ed.)
Old Owly munches.
Gobbets of torn flesh

Will this do?
T.W.

"I'm afraid he's got Odes, Mrs Keats"

Clare E. Hew

Mr Charles Moore
Is only twenty-four.
He says: "My pater and mater
are awfully pleased about me
being made Editor of the *Spectator*."

Lines on the Death of Robin Day

So. Farewell
Then Robin
Day.

(*Shome
mishtake
here shurely* –
W.D.)

Yes. You are
Right.

It should have
Been Admiral
Doenitz.

E.J. Thribb (17)

Yes, It's Harold Pinter Rhyming Slang!

Pause	Applause
Harold Pinter	Likes a classy bint... er
Homecoming	Antonia's slumming
Lady Antonia	Phonier and phonier
Cricket Blazer	Lady Antonia Fraser
	(*You've done her - Ed.*)
June 30th Group	Delightful watercress soup
NW3	Glass of sherry
Vin de Table	Margaret Drabble
CBE	Hates the bourgeoisie
Birthday Party	Hampstead arty
Sidcup	Washed up
Dumb waiter	Give me Alan Plater

In Memoriam Terry-Thomas, Old Ardinian and Comedy Star

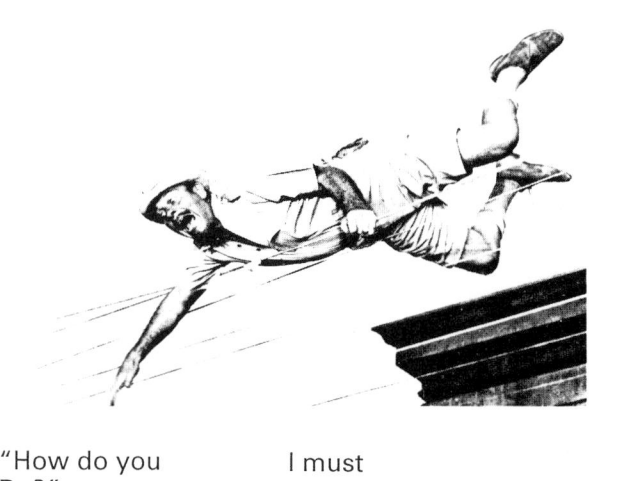

So. Farewell
Then
Terry-Thomas.

With your
Hyphen, your
Gap teeth and
Cigarette holder

You were
The quintessential
Cad.

"Absolute shower."
Yes, that was
Your catchphrase.

"How do you
Do?"
That was another.

"Good show."
That was yet
Another.

Which reminds me.

I must
Video
Those Magnificent Men
In Their
Flying Machines

When they
Put it
On.

Eric-Thribb (17½)

Lines on the Death of Philip Larkin

So. Farewell
Then Philip
Larkin

Poet
And Librarian.

Yes we
Salute you

Even though
Your output
Was small.

Your most
Famous poem
Contains a
Four letter word

Which is
Unsuitable
To repeat here.

E.J. Thribb (17)

*PS
Owing to pressure
Of space
I am unable
To include a
Tribute to
Robert Graves.*

BYZANTIUM
the
THINKING MAN'S
EURODISNEY

Yes, It's Prince Charles Rhyming Slang!

Dog and bone	Heir to the throne
Quinlan Terry	Glass of sherry
Monstrous Carbuncle	Dickie Mountbatten's your uncle
Polo player	Ozone Layer
Wholemeal toast	Laurens var der Post
Old Man of Lochnagar	Budgie the Helicopter is better by far
Standards falling	It really is appalling
Princess Diana	Upper-class manner
Thinning hair	Book of Common Prayer
Royal Duchy	Touchy
Vision of Britain	Not got much tit in

Lines on the Divorce of Janet Street-Porter

So
Farewell then
Another husband.

Number three,
Says Keith's Mum,
Who knows about
These things.

Keith does a very
Good impression
Of You.

"Harro!"

Personally, I have
Never been
Married
To you.

E.J. Thribb (17½)

Lines on the Queen's
60th Birthday

by Ted Whohes

Wolf headed magpie
Stalks black white
Black over
Flint cracked mangle
Frost-shredded
Field.

Stoat watches.

Bloodred nettle
Sprouts acid
Frond.

Old Stoatie.

Peewit shrieking
Buzzard grey
Feather drooping
Death call

Old Stoatie listens.

Swollen river
Rushes down Blood
Gorge torrent filled
Roar of white-flecked
Molten snow

Old Stoatie falls in.

Rotting stoat
Body carcass
Gleaming fish nibbled

Carrion of death
Sodden fur bulging
Eyes

Old Stoatie's
Rather had it.

Happy Birthday
Your Majesty

T.W.

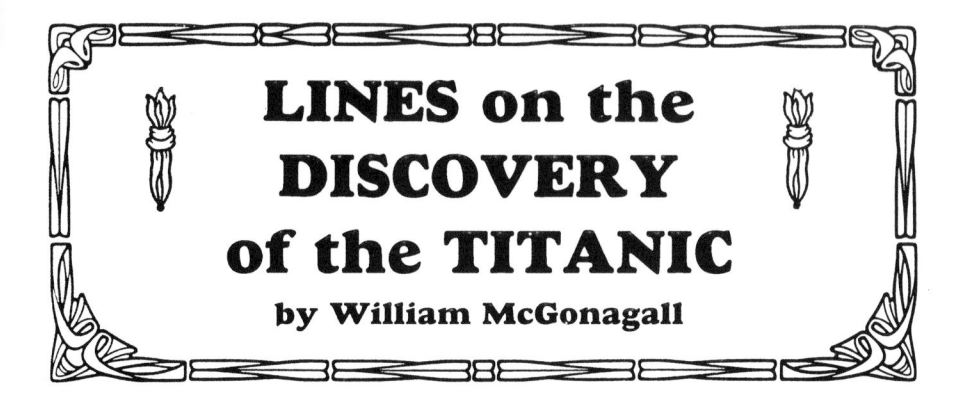

LINES on the DISCOVERY of the TITANIC

by William McGonagall

'Twas in the year nineteen hundred and eighty-five
That explorers did down to the ocean bed dive
Where they found to their amazement and panic
The wreck of the great ship they called the *Titanic*.

For seventy-three years she had lain undisturbed
With her passengers of all classes, First, Second and
                                                    Third
Down in the murky darkness, two and a half miles deep
The puir drowned folk lay in eternal sleep.

Once the *Titanic* had been the finest ship of the line
Her fittings and fixtures were gleaming and fine
But then on her maiden voyage came the terrible disaster
When an iceberg approached unseen by the Master.

Over a thousand went down to a watery grave
Though some were lucky and were saved
And until only the other day nobody had known
The exact location where the great ship went down.

Some folk would say she should be left alone
In the icy waters where she's made her home.
Relatives of the deceased have made it plain
That they don't want to see their loved ones again.

Might I put forward a plan of my own
That we should immediately call in the Heir to the Throne.
Your Royal Highness, sir, what I humbly propose
Is that you should do for the *Titanic* what you did for the
Mary Rose.

Then when the great ship comes out of the sea
It can be cleaned up and put on display
And no one will be able to understand
Why it wasn't just left lying down there in the sand.

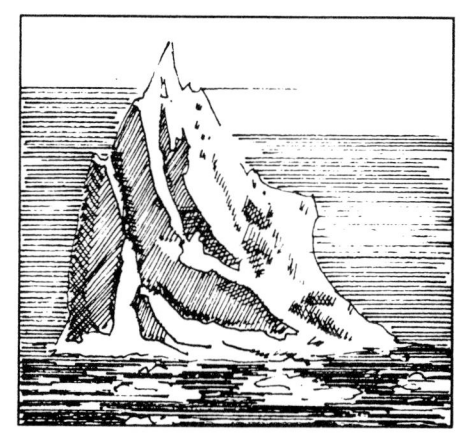

It's Indie Rhyming Slang!

Frog and Toad	City Road
Bored stiff	Whittam Smith
William Rees-Mogg	Read on the bog
Weekend Review	Nothing new
Adam Mars-Jones	Clones
Heavy type	Sunday hype
Whittam Strobes	Investigative probes
Alexander's rag	Saturday mag
Black & white cover	Steven Glover
Oliver Gillie	Willie

Lines On The Death Of Mark Boxer

So.
Farewell then
TV Anna's
Husband.

You were a
Cartoonist and
Editor.

But not on
The telly.

Which is
After all what
Matters.

E.J. Thribb (17½)

Great Moments in Poetry

Ozythatchias

by Percy Bysshe Spartey

I met a traveller on an anti-nuclear demo,
Who told me about those two amazing piles of concrete,
That apparently exist in the desert that is
Britain today.
The one is a half-finished power station, Sizewell-B by
                                                    name.
The other a half-finished tunnel under the sea near
                                                    Folkestone.
They both proclaim the legend loud and clear:
"My name is Ozythatchias,
Look upon my works, ye mighty,
And vote Labour."

Lines on the award of £55,000 in damages to Mr Robert Maxwell against Private Eye *and his earlier claim that he would "swat Mr Wigwam like a fly".*

TED WHOHES

Owd Bob

Owd Bob.
Chomping slowly
Gross belly
Sunken Eye
Owd Bob munches.

Bzzzz
Fly approaches

Bzzzz.
Owd Bob glowers
Caviar drools from
Ravenous maw

Mad eyes flame
Blood red.

Owd Bob in a strop.

Fly lights on
Owd Bob's jowl
Bzzzz.

STING.

Owd Bob
Pretty batey by this stage.

Out comes swat
Swish
Slash
Cutting through fume rich air

Owd Bob strikes.

Fly stunned drops
On loaded table
Legs in air.

Owd Bob smiles
Crack'd jaw forced open
Eyes slit
Owd Bob laughs.

Hand picks up
Fly. Into mouth it goes
Chomp Chomp
Jaws masticate dustcart-like
Garbage rich.

Burp!
Owd Bob feels better.

Bzzzz.

Fly still there buzzing
In Owd Bob's gut.

Owd Bob
Feels sick.

(Will this do? T.W.)

Lines on the Historic Agreement to Build a Channel Tunnel

by William McGonagall

'Twas in the year nineteen hundred and eighty-six
That Mrs Thatcher agreed on a link that was fixed
To join the two great nations of Britain and France:
For many of our engineers it would be their great chance.

Ever since the days of Napoleon Bonaparte
Our two fair lands had grown apart.
A stretch of ocean lay between the twain
Which could not be crossed either by car or train.

Instead it was left to the operators of ferries
Which was just as well when France was invaded by the
                                                  Jerries
For imagine what would have happened at the time of
                                                  Dunkirk:
Of his invasion Hitler would have made quick work.

But many years had passed since those darkened days
And now fair peace on both lands did gaze
And so it came about that a tunnel was once again mooted
By a number of wealthy City folk so handsomely suited.

There were many alternatives and models and mock-ups,
There was no question at all of any cock-ups.
Consortiums were formed and money was invested
By these fine gentlemen with their suits double-breasted.

Mrs Thatcher herself considered all the schemes
And the road tunnel fulfilled the idea of her dreams:
For trains she had never had any special liking
Especially when ASLEF were continually striking.

But President Mitterrand did not agree
That people should drive their cars under the sea;
He preferred High Speed Trains that huffed and puffed,
So he told Mrs Thatcher to go and get stuffed.

So the great day came at last,
In the town of Lille the die was cast.
A rail-link was to be the solution,
One advantage being the lack of pollution.

The historic announcement was finally made
Just at the same time as the resignation of the Minister of
Trade
But nobody in either country gave a toss
For they all realised the whole project was a complete dead
loss.

Lines Written Before The Election Result Was Announced To Mark The Victory Of Mrs Thatcher Or Mr Kinnock (Or Possibly Dr Owen And Mr Steel In The Event Of A Hung Parliament)

By the Poet Laureate Ted Whohes

Old wormy wriggles silently in dull earth.
Silt-rich, loam.
Cosy.
Everything fine down below.
Old wormy moves up,
Slime-trailing, eyeless, gumless, breast-heaving,
Key marginals.
Thwack.
Cold steel, sharp spade, crunch.
Old wormy equally divided.
Two wriggling, slithy, blood-gushing, guts-dropping, lumps
Of semi-dead matter.
Balance of power.
Spade flashes again.
Splat.
Wormy now in four parts.
Small swing to Scot Nats in Caithness.
Membrane, writhing, slither, viscous mess on dried oak leaf.
Splat.
Old wormy flattened by conscienceless, uncaring spade,
Ground into fine treacle of sludge.
Old Wormy not feeling too good.

Clare E. Hew

J. B. Priestley
Would never be beastly
But merely act humble
And have a good grumble.

Yes, It's Spectator Rhyming Slang!

Charles Moore	**Shown the door**
Conrad Black	**Sack**
Had enough	**Algy Cluff**
Belch	**Colin Welch**
Dominic Lawson	**Tremendous bore's son**
Vodka Tonic	**Jeff's column's chronic**
Dick West	**Past his best**
Old rope	**Wendy Cope**
Auberon Waugh	**Same as before**
Taki	**Tacky**
Bit camp	**Gavin Stamp**
Norman Stone	**Reactionary moan**
Michael Heath	**Don't understand the caption underneath**
Graham Greene	**Used to be keen**

In Memoriam

SAM COSTA

So. Farewell
Then Sam
Costa

Mustachioed Radio
Personality and
Former
Danceband Vocalist.

Keith's Mum
Remembers you
Well.

"Good morning
Sir! Was there
Something?"

That was
Your catchphrase
She says.

Was there
Something?

Yes.
But she
Has forgotten
What it was.

E.J. Thribb (17)

Lines Written On The 90th Birthday Of Her Majesty The Queen Mother

A tribute from the Poet Laureate
MR TED WHOHES

Illustration by SIR HUGE CASHIN

*I*t was in the year 1900, in the reign
of Queen Victoria
When the British empire was at its
glorious zenith,
Huge ships of iron sailed across the
seas, sic transit mundi gloria,
And Marconi was inventing the
wireless, which eventually
became a menace.

Purple heather on Glamis moor
Old grousie waits.
Grim turrets peep
Lichen-clad stone.
Gnarled beaters shout.
Earth trembles.
Old grousie flutters.

*I*t was in the year 1921
That the beautiful Lady Elizabeth
Bowes-Lyon had a lot of fun.
It was in the year King Oliver ruled
the land of jazz
And the future Queen Mother
danced the Charleston with the
young Baillie Vazz.

Leather boot crunches on peat
bog.
Barrels glint in the sun.
Hammers cock. Fingers tighten.
Sweat on lip.
Old grousie in for it any minute
now.

*I*t was in the year 1939
That Adolf Hitler sent his armies
across the Rhine.
Soon the bombs were falling on the
East End,
And the Queen Mother went down
there to become the people's friend.

Crack. Roar. Feathers flutter.
Lead on flesh. Crunch.
Blood seeps. Dogs whine.
Eyes roll. All over for old grousie.

*F*rom Hiroshima onwards we lived
in terror
In case the nuclear trigger was
pressed in error.
But throughout the years of
unending fear
Only one figure alone could bring us
cheer.

Old grousie.
(Shurely 'Queen Mother'? Ed.)
Will this do? T.W.

**Lines On The Passing
From Our Screens Of
Sir Alistair Burnet O.M.**

So. Bong!
Farewell then. Bong!
Sir Alistair Brunette. Bong!

Newscaster extraordinary.
Friend of Royalty.
Well-loved
National Institution.

"After the break – How
Freddy
The parrot tried to get a
Mortgage."

That was your catchphrase.
Bong! Ask not for whom
The bell bongs.
It bongs for
You.

I.T.N. Thribb (17½)
(*with apologies to
Ernest Hemingway*)

Clare E. Hew

Tim Rice
Is incredibly nice;
But I wouldn't complain
If he fell down a drain.

Yes, It's
Question Time
Rhyming Slang!

Peter Sissons	Never listens
Brian Lapping	No one's clapping
Sir Robin Day	Better in his day
Topical forum	How to bore 'em
On my right	Drones on all night
On my left	Sense bereft
Liberal Democrat	Old hat
Woman, token	She's hardly spoken
First-class debate	Not of late
Questions from floor	Snore
Gentleman at the back	Viewers hit sack
Lady in red	Time for bed

Lines written to mark

The Joyful Nuptials of

H.R.H. Prince Andrew

and the

"Princess Fergie"

It was in the year of 1986
That H.R.H. Prince Andrew finally got fixed
So he chose as his bride the redheaded Fergie
Who some said resembled a drawing by the Tintin artist Hergé.

For many years the young Prince had sowed his wild oats
Taking girls with him on aeroplanes and in boats.
Dallying with them became something of a habit
As was discovered one afternoon by Miss Katy Rabbitt.

Most famous of all was the actress Koo Stark
Who would never say no to a bit of a lark
But when it was learned that she had appeared naked on the
                                                                screen
It did not amuse Her Majesty the Queen.

It was then that the Duke had a word in Andrew's ear:
"At least, my boy, it shows that you are not a queer.
An actress is fine for a bit on the side,
But you must find someone else to be your bonny bride."

Now it so chanced that the Duke had a very good friend
With whom he played polo every weekend.
Major Ronald Ferguson was his name
And his daughter Sarah had beautiful long hair like flame.

When this red-haired lovely caught the eye of the Prince
He said: "Fergie, my dear, my words I won't mince.
My pater has told me I must settle down
Because I am fourth in line to the crown."

And so it was agreed that the whole nation should stand by
For a royal wedding on the 23rd of July
But Mrs Thatcher as usual behaved like a Turk
And decreed that everyone should still go to work.

But when at last the bells rang out
There were very few people about.
They were all staying at home to watch the event on TV
Thus giving the traditional two-fingers to Mrs T.

Clare E. Hew

Mr Dennis Skinner
Is not the sort of chap you'd have to dinner
But he certainly has his use
If you want vulgar jibes and abuse.

WORDSWORTH
POP-UP
BOOK

Lines on the First
Anniversary of
Mr Murdoch's
Sky Television

So.
Farewell then
Sky Television.

You are
One.

As is
Your
Audience.

B.S.B. Thribb (17½)

Yes, It's Nigel Kennedy Rhyming Slang!

Brahms and Liszt	Platinum disc
Bruch and Viv	Spiv
Bach's Air	Silly hair
Leather jacket	Makes a packet
Stephan Grappelli	Trainers, smelly
Berlin Philharmonic	Looks moronic
Supports Aston Villa	Uses words like 'killer!'
Stradivarius	Thinks he's hilarious
Friend of Gazza's	Appeals to the mazzes
Toured with the Hallé	Bit of a wally
Violincello	Tiresome fellow
Quattro Stagione	Street cred's phoney
Studied with Menuhin	Accent's not genuine
Kennedy, Nige	'E's all the rige

Lines On The
Death of
St Malcolm
of Muggeridge,
Journalist,
Broadcaster,
Sage and Onion

So. Farewell then
Malcolm Muggeridge.

"More and more as
            I grow older"
"When some future
            Gibbon"
"What could be more
            ludicrous?"
"Irredeemably
            mediocre"
"The whole show's over"
"All washed up"

Yes. Those were your
Catchphrases.

Keith's Mum said
That you were
Always saying
That you wanted to die.

Now, at last,
Your wish has been
Granted.

E.J. Thribb (87½)

Lines on the 70th Birthday of the Duke of Edinburgh

by Mr Ted Whohes, Poet Laureate

Old Pit Bull
Snarls on leather
Leash. Brass studded
Teeth bared. Jaws slaver.

Old Himmler waits.

Tied to lamppost
On dirty street.
Owner lager-filled in
Sweaty pub.
Sawdust feet, NF tattoo
On flexed muscle.
Torn T-shirt.

Old Himmler broods.

Leash slipped,
Old Himmler away.
Pounding, padding.
Jaws lock,
Biting fury, trousers rent.
Mr Patel taken to Casualty.

Old Himmler does it again.

Happy Birthday,
Your Royal Highness.

Lines Composed In Honour of the Great Battle That Was Held To Commemorate the First Anniversary of the Opening of the Fortress of Wapping

'Twas in the year nineteen hundred and eighty-seven
That folk came from as far away as Devon
To take part in a mighty celebration
That took the form of a spontaneous demonstration.

At their head stood the proud figure of Brenda Dean,
Of the printworkers of Britain she was the queen.
The ranks of SOGAT there seemed no stopping
As they converged *en masse* on Fortress Wapping.

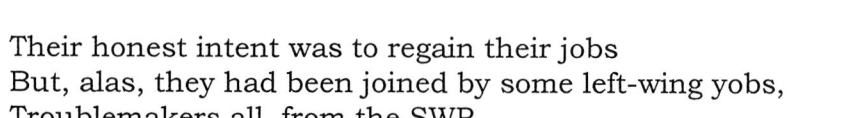

Their honest intent was to regain their jobs
But, alas, they had been joined by some left-wing yobs,
Troublemakers all, from the SWP,
Including, 'twas said, members of Paul Foot's family.

As night came on and the sky grew blacker
There appeared hundreds of horsemen led by Inspector
                                                    Knacker.
Soon with cries of "Pig" the air was thick
Not to mention many a well-aimed brick.

In vain did poor Brenda appeal for calm.
As Dennis Skinner MP tried to raise the alarm.
Soon the armies were on collision course,
Both the demonstrators and the Metropolitan Police Force.

Caught in the melee was the lovely Kate Adie,
The BBC's most beautiful reporting lady,
Who was soon giving the viewers of the nation
A first-hand report of this shocking demonstration.

It was clear that by now the ranks of each army
Had gone what we doctors call "completely barmy".
No one noticed, while they were committing their crimes,
That Rupert Murdoch was quietly getting on with printing
                              several million copies of
            the *News of the World* and the *Sunday Times*.

© W. McGonagall 1987

The Lion And The Unicorn

Unicorn. Gentle
Erect, vulnerable.
Grazing.
Silver horn glistens
In sun.
Corkscrew-like.

Lion in bushes.
Golden mane, mangy
Roar.
Spring. Rip. Tear.
Teeth sink into soft belly.

Unicorn squeals.
Too late. Blood, guts.
Gush. Grisly.
Lion chews.
Only horn left.

Happy anniversary,
Ma'am.

(*Is this bad
enough? TW*)

IN MEMORIAM

Lines on the announcement that Miss Samantha Fox is to retire from Page Three modelling

So. Farewell
Then Samantha
Fox.

Or at least
Part of
You.

You are going
To be
A pop star.

Keith says
You are no
Good.

But that never
Stopped anyone
Before.

E.J. Thribb (17½)

Clare E. Hew

BRAIN OF BRITAIN

Lady Diana Spencer
Was not a member of Mensa.
Had she been brighter
She wouldn't have married the blighter.

Yes, It's Sissinghurst Rhyming Slang!

Vita Sackville-West	**Likes women best**
Violet Trefusis	**Never refuses**
Moustache tickles 'em	**Harold Nicolson**
Nigel Nicolson	**Rather a fickle son**
National Trust	**Terrific bust**
Soft porn	**Ornamental lawn**
Potting shed	**Two-in-a-bed**
Nasturtium	**Perversion**
Naked breasts	**Sackville-Wests**
Country hikes	**Designer dykes**
Cor! Phew!	**BBC2**
Nicolson, Senior	**Could have been queenier**
Nicolson, Junior	**Getting loonier**

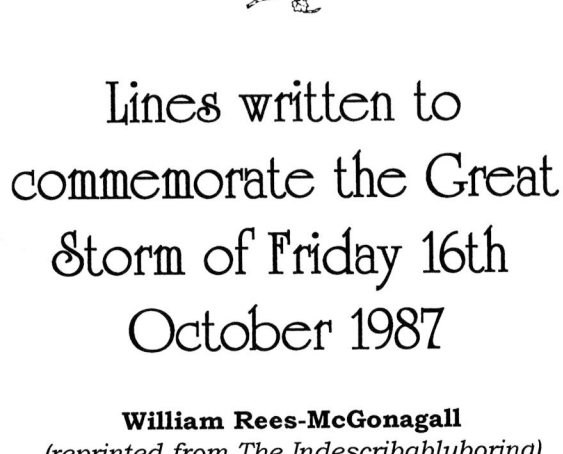

Lines written to commemorate the Great Storm of Friday 16th October 1987

William Rees-McGonagall
(reprinted from The Indescribablyboring)

’Twas in October of the year nineteen
                 hundred and eighty-seven
That an almighty storm came down from
                       heaven.
The hurricane came completely out of the blue
And the fact that it was coming nobody knew.

❖

The whole population was tucked up in bed
When suddenly the tempest roared over their
                       head.
Like a raging lion, it roared and roared
While most of the people just slept and snored.

❖

But when they awoke they saw scenes of
                       devastation
Which had laid waste almost the whole of the
                       nation.
At least this was true in Sussex and Kent
Where many a greenhouse got rather bent.

❖

Huge trees were uprooted and fell over the roads
Lorries on the M25 were reported to have
                                shed their loads,
Meanwhile many a home was deprived of power
Which made it in every sense Britain's
                                darkest hour.

❖

Millions were unable to get to work
And this was not because they wished to shirk,
But when they set out to catch the 8.23
They found the way was barred by an
                                enormous tree.

❖

Then out came the chain saws and the strong
                                cups of char
As neighbours spoke to each other for the
                                first time since the war.
They all pulled together as they had done in
                                the Blitz
Instead of sitting around looking at pictures of
                                page 3 tits.

❖

And everywhere there was only one topic of
                                every conversation
Among every section of the population.
As they began to search for someone to blame
They all soon agreed that it was the Met men's
                                night of shame.

❖

"Why weren't we told?" went up the cry
(Though how this would have helped, no one
                                could descry).
And at last the British people had only one
                                universal wish,
The public execution of Messrs McCaskill and
                                Fish.

Clare E. Hew

The Reverend Jesse Jackson
Seems to turn the blacks on
But he's not such good news
For the Jews.

Lines on the departure of Derek Jameson from his Radio Two morning programme, by mutual agreement with the BBC

So. Farewell
Then,
Derek Jameson.

You have
Been sacked.

"Blimey!"

That was
Your catchphrase.

"Here are the
New Seekers."

That was
Another.

E.J. Thribb (17½)

In Memoriam
Sergio Leone

So. Farewell
Then
Sergio Leone.

Famed director
Of Spaghetti
Westerns.

A Fistful Of
Dollars. That
Was your first.

For A Few
Dollars More.

Terrific.

The Good, The
Bad And The
Ugly. That
Was another masterpiece.

When I heard
You had
Died, my first
Thought was:

Great. They will
All be on TV
Again.

E.J. "Clint" Thribb (17½)

LINES WRITTEN TO COMMEMORATE THE 200TH BIRTHDAY
OF THE NOBLE COUNTRY OF AUSTRALIA

It was in the year 1774
That there first arrived on this fatal shore
The *Endeavour*, a ship of Captain Cook's,
Which fourteen years later was followed by a boatload of crooks.

They arrived in the year 1788,
200 years ago, so I calculate.
In England they'd been found guilty of stealing many a sheep,
And so in its wisdom the government decided to transport them across the
deep.

So they arrived in Botany Bay,
Where the natives espied them and quickly ran away.
It was a harsh land that now met their view,
Populated by the platypus and the kangaroo.

It did not take these felons more than a few years
To discover gold and invent lager beers.
They forged a new nation, proud and tough,
While the poor wee abos pranced around in the buff.

In the years since then they have produced many famous names,
Like Sir Donald Bradman and Clive James.
The other celebrities have all come over here:
I am thinking of Rolf Harris and Germaine Greer.

I could also deliver a very long lecture
On Australian achievements in the field of architecture,
Such as the Sydney Opera House and the Harbour Bridge,
Both often mentioned by Dame Edna Everage.

Of outdoor sports they have not a few,
Ending every day on the beach with a bar-b-cue.
Waltzing Matilda is their favourite tune,
And the men wear hats with corks hanging doon.

So let us join with the Prince and Princess of Wales,
And the Tall Boats in the harbour with their billowing sails,
All gathered together in Commemoration
To celebrate the birth of this wonderful nation.

No one can say this Experiment has been
a failure,
Which is why we all sing Happy Birthday
Australia.

© **WILLIAM MCGONAGALL**

Lines on the 20th Anniversary of the *Sun* Newspaper

So. Hats off
Then.
The soaraway
Sun.

You are
Twenty.

"There's more
Fun in the
Sun."

That is
Your catchphrase.

Unfortunately,
Like everything
Else in the
Sun,

This is
Not true.

E.J. Thribb
(17½ –34½ –17½)

Yes, It's Inspector Morse Rhyming Slang!

Wednesday night	Viewer's delight
Two-hour slot	Impenetrable plot
Another case	Very slow pace
News at Ten after	Should get a BAFTA
TV dinner	Franchise winner
Morse, Inspector	Money for Colin Dexter
John Thaw	He gets even more
Kevin Whately	Made quite a bit lately
Sergeant Lewis	Loved by reviewers
Oxford location	Pleasant vacation
Murder and robbery	Plenty of snobbery
Opera buff	That's enough (*Ed.*)

In Memoriam
Lines on the death of Sammy Davis Jr

So farewell then
Sammy Davis Jr.

Mr Wonderful they
Called you.

But who was
Sammy Davis Sr?

That is the
Really interesting
Question.

E.J. Thribb (17½)

Clare E. Hew

Robert Maxwell
Avoids paying tax well
Like many greedy swine
He registers his companies in Liechtenstein.

Lines on the Marriage of His Royal Highness the Prince Andrew & Miss Sarah Ferguson

Black clouds mass
Over Mulroney Fell
Ground shakes
Snout opens
Moley surfaces

Velvet periscope
Scans bracken
Claws scuffle
Mossy earth

Moley the watchful

Blind eyes
Gloved head
Peering

Thunder threatens
As Moley waits
From torrid sky
Hawk

Dives
Dives
Dives

Feathered bullet
Smashes through
Fur, skull
Blood, crushed bone

Moley rather
Washed up.

T. Whohes © 1986

Yes, It's Gulf Crisis Rhyming Slang

F.O.	Didn't know
Kuwait	Too late
Saudi	Howdy!
Arab sheik	Knees quake
Baghdad	Raving mad
Quite insane	Saddam Hussein
Moustache and beret	Bonkers, very
Facial hair	Germ warfare
Persian Gulf	Worse than Adolf
Massive army	Barmy
Jihad	Looking bad
George Bush	Big push
US ships	Read my lips
F-111	Get to heaven
Peter Snow	'Ere we go

ODE on MELANCHOLY

DEJECTION SLIP

Clare E. Hew

Tam Dalyell
Is as famous as hell;
But what I want to know
Is who on earth was General Belgrano?

Lines on the Historic Occasion of the Official Dinner given in The White House to say Farewell to President Reagan

Composed by Mr William McGonagall

'Twas in the month of November in 1988
    That the great President Reagan decided to celebrate,
For he knew that he would have to retire in 1989,
    And that is why he invited Mrs Thatcher over to dine.

It would be hard to imagine a more glittering scene,
    Unless the occasion had been graced by Her Majesty The Queen.
The great ones of the nation stood patiently in line
    To toast their beloved President in Californian wine.

O! What a host of geniuses had assembled together,
    Led by the greatest composer in the world, Andrew Lloyd Webber,
And also the great novelist, seated on Mrs Reagan's right,
    Mr Thomas Wolfe, in his famous suit so white.

And, fresh from his much-acclaimed retrospective at the Tate,
    Came Mr David Hockney, with a small blond mate.
The preacher Billy Graham did not know what to say,
    He had never before sat at dinner with a gay.

There then fell on the company a might hush
    As there entered the President Elect, George Bush.
But the President's staff had neglected to mail
    An invitation to the Vice-President Elect, J. Danforth Quayle.

Finally the lights dimmed at the climax of the ball
    For the entrance of the most glittering guest of all.
When it came to glamour there was no one to match
    The radiant figure of Mrs Margaret Thatch.

A mighty cheer rose up from the throng,
    It was what they had been waiting for all along:
The sight of the greatest stateswoman the world has known,
    Who specially from Gatwick that morning had flown.

As she stood before them in all her glory,
    Everyone present wished they too could have voted Tory.
What did it matter that they were losing Ron —
    When the immortal Iron Lady would go on and on and on?

Lines Written To Celebrate The Historic Completion Of The Channel Tunnel*

by Sir William Rees-McGonagall

(or at least the 2" borehole linking the French and British service ducts)

'Twas in the year nineteen hundred nine and zero
That Mr Alistair Morton became the nation's hero.
For he was the Chairman of Eurotunnel plc
That dug a mighty hole all the way under the sea.

For millions of years the island of Albion had stood alone
Reachable only by Sealink and Vodaphone
Cut off from Europe by a strait of twenty-two miles.
No wonder Shakespeare had called it one of the most sceptred of
                                                              isles.

Proudly the islanders looked out from the White Cliffs of Dover
Telling the Europeans that they could not come over.
Many were the invaders who sailed in vain —
Napoleon, Caesar, Saxon and Dane.

And we must not forget the Spanish Armada,
If there had been no Channel, Drake's job would have been harder.
And let us not forget either the designs of Hitler
Who would have goosestepped up Whitehall if the Channel had been
                                                              littler.

But eventually a new age dawned, an era of peace,
When businessmen needed to travel from Glasgow to Greece.
So President Mitterrand got together with Mrs Thatch,
And a great plan for a tunnel they began to hatch.

Canterbury Cathedral was the historic venue.
And now we can tell you what was on the menu.
Frogs Legs and Brown Windsor Soup were the choice of starters,
Or, for those who didn't like either of these things, the juice of
tomatoes.

The main course followed — Roast Lamb from Wales,
And from the French, of course, six escargots, also known as snails.
A variety of sweets was served from the trolley —
Profiteroles or Christmas Pudding with holly.

After lunch they signed the historic accord
Perhaps because of all the brandy and liqueurs they had taken on
board.
And from that day forth the huge machines began to bore,
Making a gigantic hole beneath the ocean floor.

But things did not turn out to be altogether sunny
As Mr Morton's consortium kept on running out of money.
Cap in hand, he would return to his backers,
Who began to realise the whole idea was crackers.

But there was no stopping the redoubtable Mr Morton
As with Churchillian courage he gallantly fought on.
And at last in October came the moment long awaited
As the people of Europe watched with breath a-bated.

Finally the Continent and Britain were joined.
"Well Done Maggie," was the phrase the *Daily Mail* coined.
It seemed that the tunnellers had achieved their goal,
But in fact they had only made a very small hole.

No sooner had the champagne corks ceased to pop
Than the penny with the public began to drop.
They realised that the project was far from done:
The digging of the tunnel itself hadn't yet begun.

IN MEMORIAM

John Arlott, Cricket Commentator

So. Farewell
Then.

John Arlott.

The Voice
Of Summer,

As you were
Dubbed.

"And after
Trevor Bailey
It will be
Christopher
Martin-Jenkins."

That was
Your
Catchphrase.

But who can
There be
After you?

E.J. Thribb (17½ not out)

Clare E. Hew

The Bhaghwan Rajneesh
Is incredibly reech.
Even Gawd
Is overawed.

**In Memoriam
Lymeswold Cheese
1982–1992**

So. Farewell
Then.

Lymeswold.

Yes, you
Are going
Out of
Production.

Hard cheese.

Or, rather,
Soft cheese.

In your
Case

E.J. Thribb (17½)

Great Moments in Poetry Revisited

OZYTHATCHIAS

By Percy Bysshe Spartey

I met a traveller on the Jubilee line
Who said: A vast tower of concrete
Stands in the Docklands. Near it lie
Idle cranes and empty offices.
And on the pedestal these words appear:
"My name is Ozythatchias,
Supreme Ruler of the Universe.
Look on my works, ye mighty, and despair."
Nothing beside remains. Round the decay
Of that colossal wreck, boundless and bare,
The lone and level sand and cement
Mixers stretch far away.

by William Rees-McGonagall

Lines Written On The Occasion Of The Historic Victory Of Mr Graham Gooch Against The West Indies At Leeds

'Twas in the summer of Nineteen Hundred and Ninety-One
When there was plenty of rain but not much sun
That the most historic test match ever was played
Whose glorious memory will never fade.

From the Caribbean Sea came a mighty side
Whose cricketing skill was famed both far and wide.
There was no team in the world they could not beat
As many of them towered up over ten feet.

At their very names the English hearts froze —
Patterson, Walsh, Marshall and Curtly Ambrose.
And this was only to speak of their bowling attack
Without reckoning how hard the ball their batsmen could whack.

Richardson, Richards, Logie and Dujon —
When it came to sixes, each of them could hit a huge one.
No wonder poor Gooch thought his team would lose
And probably end up covered with many a bruise.

Few could remember the last time England had won,
It was way back in the Sixties, when the PM was Wilson.
At that time men were setting foot on the moon
And ever since England had taken the wooden spoon.

But this time what a wondrous change was wrought
As every catch by the English fielders was caught —
Gooch, Hick, Atherton and Ramprakash:
Among the newcomers the latter cut a particular dash.

Many times the weather threatened to intervene
As over the ground huge black clouds were seen.
Many was the time the West Indians appealed against the light
But Umpire Dicky Bird said, "Play on, it is quite all right."

On the first morning as eleven o'clock struck
Everyone thought Gooch and Atherton would soon be out for a duck.
In the event the first over was fine
As the new ball in the hands of Ambrose began to lose its shine.

Then Atherton played on a quick one from Patterson.
Back in the pavilion they all said, "What's the matter, son?"
(*The next 307 verses of ball-by-ball poetry have been omitted for reasons of space.*)

And thus Gooch was not out for one hundred and fifty-four,
Batting right through the innings, which had only been done four
                                                    times before.
By Geoffrey Boycott, to name but one
And another, of course, was Sir Leonard Hutton.
(*Another 761 verses relating to famous records have been omitted. Full text on Gnomefax p.94.*)

Oh 'twas a famous victory for Gooch and his men —
We shall never see its like again —
And everyone in England felt astonishingly proud,
Especially the seven wet spectators who were in the crowd.

VERSES BY WENDY COPE (The next Poetess Laureate)

The Poetess At Last Recognises Her True Worth

The editor phoned and asked me
Is your name Wendy Cope?
Would you take some money
For a yard of old rhyming rope?

I said, "When do you want it?"
He said, "As fast as you can do"
I said, "I'll start just as soon as
I've downed a bottle or two"

The editor said he'd like them
About all the usual stuff:
Lunch and bad weather and poets
And boyfriends cutting up rough

And having one too many
And feeling rather down
And having another too many
Vide: "Tears of a Clown"

But when I quoted my prices
He said that cash was tight;
And instead he'd print Dorothy Parker
Who was no longer in copyright.

Why I Put Men In My Poems

I often write about men
And how they let you down
Which is all very handy
Because "down" rhymes with "frown"
And "noun" and "crown" and "town".

I also like the word "men"
Because it rhymes with "wren"
And "then" and "den" and "pen".
So I write to all the editors
Saying would you like a poem
about men
— Again?
They say, "Yes, but could you make
it scan
This time?"
I say, "Of course I can make it scan
and I can also make
It rhyme."
So they cough
And let me off.

Another Poem About Men

I look in the fridge
And find it empty
But nothing rhymes with empty
So I look again
And find a hen
Which gives me the chance
To make this another poem about men.

Why Are Other Poets So Glum With Me?

Why are other poets so glum with me?
Where are their poetic loyalties?
Why do they grow snappy
And so very unhappy
Whenever I mention my royalties?

Which If Any Great Poets Might I Have Fancied?

I suppose I could have fancied Milton
Though his feet might smell of Stilton
Or maybe I could have gone for Keats
If he'd been better between the sheets
I could have had a date with Kipling
But his muscles were far from rippling
Dylan Thomas could have made me
                             frisky
If his breath hadn't smelt of whisky
A crush on Shakespeare, I might have
                            fear'd,
If it wasn't for that awful beard
I might have gone for Rupert Brooke
But he had that awful pansy look
And I couldn't take the loopy stare
Of the also-bearded mad John Clare
And the creepiest guy around
Must surely be old Ezra Pound
Wordsworth and his daffodils
Could never give me the thrills
And the great Alexander Pope
Doesn't appeal to Wendy Cope
Leaving me with Edith Sitwell
Which doesn't make me feel a bit well.

What Do You Think?

A man called Desmond
A bloke called Ron
A boy called Andrew
A guy called John
They all vanished, for better or worse
And all I had asked them
Was what they thought of my verse.

Buses I Have Written Poems To Past Lovers On In The Past Fortnight

56, 14, 29, 11,
19, 23, 24, 8.
17, 8, 44, 7,
4, 12, 18 (late).

Without A Punchline

Just occasionally, I write poems which
Don't have any sort of rhyme at all.
Instead, they just meander on
And then finish without a punchline.

Things I Must Do Today

Fetch my laundry
Darn my socks
Put my old sheets
In a box.
Have a drink,
Make some toast.
Go shopping for
The Sunday roast.
Watch some telly
Sip some tea
Give the milkman
Thirty pee.
What a lot
Of boring labour
But apparently not
To the man at Faber.

                                 W. C.

Lines On The Passing Of The Right Honourable Margaret Hilda Thatcher, PM

by Sir William Rees-McGonagall

'Twas in the year 1990, on the 22nd of November —
That will be a date for everyone to remember,
For it was on that day Mrs Thatcher was forced to resign
After a surprisingly good showing in the first ballot by Mr Heseltine.

It all began in the House of Commons a few days earlier
When Sir Geoffrey Howe spoke, he had never looked surlier.
MPs crowded in to hear his historic oration
Which could also, thanks to Mr Baird's televisual device, be
witnessed by the entire nation.

At his words the Tories were utterly aghast
For they knew now that Mrs Thatcher might soon be breathing her last.
The Labour Party the Red Flag began to sing,
And Mr Heseltine threw his hat into the ring.

At once the nation was on the edge of its seat
As they watched the inimitable (shurely incomprehensible?) John Cole
talking in the street.
"Hondootedly Mossis Thotcher," that was his familiar catch-phrase
Which he was to go on repeating for many days.

At the stroke of 6, the result came through:
Mrs Thatcher 204, Mr Heseltine 152.
Although it seemed that Mrs Thatcher had won
According to the rules, the contest had scarcely begun.

As Mr Heseltine's supporters broke into a dance
The news was relayed to Mrs Thatcher in Paris, France.
She rushed down the steps, after a quick glass of gin,
And shouted to Mr John Sergeant: "I fight on, I fight to win."

Her pledge that she would battle on for another day
Was greeted by senior Tories with dismay.
The members of her Cabinet were soon in cahoots
And Mrs Thatcher had a visit from the men in grey suits.

The message they gave her was loud and clear:
"We appreciate what you've done, but you are no longer welcome
here."
And so it was on the day of November 22nd
Something happened which nobody had ever reckoned.

Mrs Thatcher announced that she would have to go
Which came as a great shock to both friend and foe.
Mr Cole was still talking in the street outside
Explaining that the contest was now open wide.

"Hondootedly," he said, the front-runners would be Major and Hurd,
The former being someone of whom few had ever heard.
Now the race was on to see who could replace Mrs Thatcher
While TV's Charles Moore said there was no one to match her.

For three days there was nothing to be viewed on the screen
Except the three candidates saying how against the poll tax they had
always been.
The betting shops were meanwhile taking many a wager
As the odds continued to shorten on Mr John Major.

Finally at 6.00 Big Ben began to sound
And Mr Cranley Onslow read out the result of the second round.
To the astonishment of all the chattering classes
They'd elected some chap in a suit and glasses.

Thus ended an historical chapter in the nation's story
Bringing a tear to the eye of many a Tory,
Particularly to readers of the Daily Telegraph —
While everyone else enjoyed a jolly good laugh.

Lines Written On The Funeral Of
The Late Captain Robert Maxwell MC

'Twas in the year nineteen hundred and ninety-one
That occurred the tragic death of Israel's greatest son.
Known to all the world as Robert Maxwell,
The mysterious circumstances of his end served all the hacks well.

But however amazing was the way he drowned,
It was as nothing compared with the ceremony when he was put in
the ground.
A State Funeral, no less, was decreed by Prime Minister Shamir
And great leaders came from both far and from near.

And so outside the walls of the Holy City
The great crowd gathered, weeping with pity.
There were dignitaries too many to count,
All solemnly assembled on the Olive Mount.

Shamir and Sharon and Gerald Kaufmann too.
Even Archbishop Coggan joined that motley crew,
Which was led to the graveside by President Herzog.
(The only person missing was William Rees-Mogg.)

Before the corpse into the ground was laid
Many a tribute to the deceased was paid
(Unlike the bills he had left behind —
A vast sum indeed for his poor sons to find!).

They spoke of him as a hero and a saint,
Which to some observers he certainly ain't (*shurely 'wasn't'? Ed.*)
As a mixture of Churchill and Moses, they described this tycoon,
With no one saying that he was a bullying buffoon.

And so fittingly he returned to his native land
(Where he had never actually lived, on the other hand).
But it was appropriate he should rest at last in the land of milk
and honey,
For, after all, he had given them an awful lot of money.

© William Rees-McGonagall, 1991

Yes, It's Viscount Althorp Rhyming Slang!

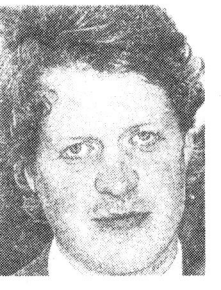

Sally Ann Lasson	**Night of passion**
Di's brother	**Bit of the other**
Society Beauty	**Not very fruity**
Kiss 'n' tell	**Paris hotel**
Dinner at Claridges	**Not good for marriages**
Bit of wallop	***Tatler* trollop**
Rumpy-Pumpy	**Now she's grumpy**
Five grand	**One night stand**
Romantic sex	**Large cheques**
News of the World	**Toes curled**
Victoria Lockwood	**Dump him, she should**
Charlie	**Charlie**

Lines on the Disintegration of the Soviet Union

So. Farewell
Then
Mikhail Gorbachev.

Famous Russian
Leader.

Glasnost.

That was
Your catchphrase.

Perestroika.

That was
Another.

Gizzajob.

That could
Be your new
One.

E.J. Thribb (17½)

Clare E. Hew

Naim Attallah
Is a funny colour.
Quite good for his age –
Sort of indigo-beige.

Lines Written to Commemorate the Closure of Punch

by William Rees-McGonagall

'Twas in the year Eighteen Hundred and Forty-One
That the great magazine *Punch* was first begun.
Many humorists of the time contributed to its pages,
Though not Charles Dickens, who was used to working for rather
higher wages.

By the year Eighteen Hundred and Forty-Three
People began to say "It is not as funny as it used to be."
And so it continued through the long reign of Victoria
When one of its most famous cartoonists was Sir George Du Maurier
(And even then it was known as "the magazine guaranteed to bore yer").

When Edward VII came in due course to the throne
The weekly arrival of *Punch* was greeted with a groan.
Then came George V to guide the nation
But still the magazine maintained its healthy circulation.

What was the reason for this extraordinary feat?
The answer lay in the waiting rooms of Wimpole Street.
There piled high for the patients to see
Were hundreds of copies of the London Charivari.

The dental profession continued to give it unfailing support,
Even though the readership among the rest of the population was nought.
And so it continued for many decades more,
A national institution that only sufferers from neuralgia actually saw.

By this time easily the best-known feature of *Punch*
Was the table at which the wits sat around for lunch.
On it were carved the names of many famous men,
Such as the Duke of Edinburgh and Mr Anthony Wedgwood Benn.

Year after year *Punch* continued to
    induce a deep slumber,
Particularly with its special annual
    Motor Show Number.
Other features which failed to hold
    the attention
Were "*Punch* On Food" and "A
    Special Humorous Supplement On
    Your Home Extension".

Among the many contributors whose
    work was not enjoyed
Were William Davis, Alan Coren, Roy
    Hattersley, Hunter Davies, Lord
Mancroft and Sir Clement Freud.
Among other tedious columnists
    who performed yeoman service
Were Sheridan Morley and Radio 4's
    Libby Purves.

But then at last the penny finally
    dropped
And the subscriptions from the
    dentists suddenly stopped.
After more than a century of giving it
    their money
They realised that *Punch* had never
    actually been funny.

The owners of *Punch* did not know
    what to do
As they saw the disappearance of
    their revenue.
So the men in suits hired a member
    of the younger generation,
And made him the editor in the hope
    of recovering their circulation.

However this did not prove a very
    good bet
As David Thomas proved to be the
    least funny editor yet.
Despite a publicity campaign costing
    a million and a half,
Punch had to close down, finally
    giving everyone a good laugh.

Classic Cartoons from the Archives

TRUE HUMILITY
The Curate. "OH NO, MY LORD, I ASSURE YOU! PARTS OF IT ARE EXCELLENT!"

THE MAN WHO FOUND *PUNCH* FUNNY

THE BRITISH CHARACTER
"FAILURE TO FIND *PUNCH* AMUSING"

MODERN NONSENSE RHYMES

(Believed to relate to the victory of BSkyB in
the Auction of Televised Football in 1992)

Hey Diddle Diddle

The Fat Cat's on the fiddle.

Murdoch is over the moon.

The watchdog failed to stop the fun

And the Dish ran away with the football.

Anon.

Lines To Commemorate The Possible Rift In The Marriage Of Their Royal Highnesses, The Prince And Princess Of Wales.

by The Poet Laureate

Old Warthog Drinks
Mudhole running dry. Snuffling snout.

Grunt. Groan.
Dirt-caked skin. Piggy eyes stare.

Old Warty pretty hot .
Flea bites. Pain sears.

Warty scratches ear
With cleft foot.
Brain maddened. Dance
Of frenzy.

Warty has heart attack.
Keels over.
Poor old Warty.

Will This Do? Ted Whohes

In Memoriam
**Frankie Howerd
and Benny Hill**

So. Farewell
Then

Benny Hill.

You did not
Have a
Catchphrase.

"Titter ye
Not."

That was
Frankie Howerd's.

No, we shall
Not titter on
This solemn
Occasion.

E.J. Thribb (17½)

Yes, It's Maastricht Rhyming Slang!

Maastricht	**Major's arse licked**
Lubbers, Ruud	**UK screwed**
F-word	**Douglas Hurd**
John Major	**Bit of a failure**
Wim Kok	**Unfortunate name for the DutchFinance Minister**
EMU	**Sod you**
Social Charter	**Non-starter**
Jacques Delors	**Terrific bore**
Mitterrand	**Ennui, grand**
Opt-out clause	**Up yours**
Britain's arse licked	**Maastricht**

IN MEMORIAM
NOTHING IN
PARTICULAR

So. No one important
Has died
In the past few days.

Nor, for that matter
Has anyone famous
Had a birthday.

Such things are sent
To try the poet.

E. Jarvis Tharb (17)